Why I'm Blessed to Have You As A Friend

The little things that mean a lot

Sharron Stockhausen

ISBN 1-931945-24-1

Library of Congress Catalog Number: 2004095942

Printed in Korea

First Printing: September 2004

08 07 06 05 04   6 5 4 3 2 1

Expert Publishing, Inc.
14314 Thrush Street NW, Andover, MN 55304-3330
1-877-755-4966
www.ExpertPublishingInc.com

Acknowledgements

No one writes a book alone, and I am no exception. Since I cannot prioritize the importance of the contributions of my friends, suffice it to say I thank all my friends whose impact on my life is mentioned in this book. Each one of you inspired me for your own special reason. You will all find yourselves in here if you just read this book.

I am extremely blessed to have my best friend also be my husband, Harry. There is no doubt in my mind or heart that God provided Harry especially for me. I am confident no other man would have been so patient with me these many decades.

My adult children taught me many lessons about friendship over the years. Stacy showed me how mother and daughter can become very close friends, even though we haven't always understood each other. Eric amazed me with his ability to create—and keep—lifelong friends from grade school, through college, and into becoming spouses and parents, even while thousands of miles separate him from his friends. Eric's wife, Sally, taught me the joy of having a daughter-in-law who loves the son we raised as much as we do. What a blessing.

Finally, I must thank my writers group, Dr. Bill Klein, Wayne Adams, and Carolyn Roles, and illustrator, Cindy Brueck, for sharing my dream to show the world why I am blessed by the friends in my life. The group's critique and comments added so much. And the creativity behind the illustrations is immeasurable. More blessings.

You accept me as I am.

*You boost my confidence
when I'm feeling
a little shaky.*

You understand that
sometimes I need
quiet time alone.

You let me go on the telephone the first time I tell you, "I have to go."

You smile whenever

you see me.

You come over
for tea on occasion.

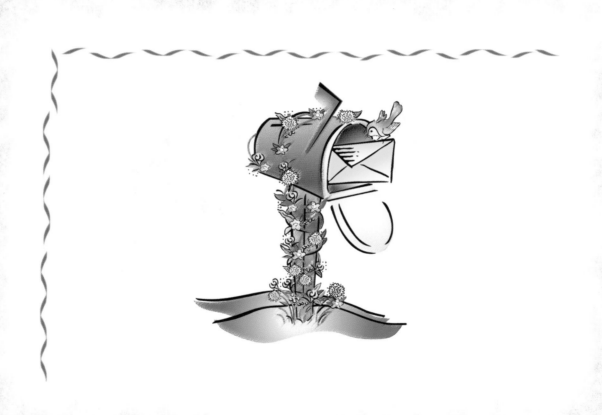

You send me greeting cards on holidays other than Christmas.

You invite me to go places like the theater with you.

*You bring me vegetables
from your garden.*

*You feed my pet
when I'm out of town.*

You bring me some of your homemade soup whenever you make it.

You give me gifts
to encourage me
to pamper me.

You pray for me.

*You make me
feel appreciated.*

You hug me.

You bring me flowers for no particular reason.

You treat me to lunch
once in awhile and
let me reciprocate.

You aren't afraid to tell me what I need to hear.

*You remember
my birthday.*

You take classes with me even when you're not interested in the subject.

You always make sure
I'm never alone
on the holidays.

You listen without offering unsolicited advice.

You go to garage sales with me without judging what I buy.

You allow me time away from you when I need it.

You congratulate me when I lose a few pounds.

*You never mention it
when I gain them back.*

*You ask my opinion on
things important to you.*

*You come to my
celebrations.*

You give me perfect gifts, those you've put some thought into.

You share memories we've made along the way.

You never say, "I told you so," even when you told me so.

*You cry with me
when I'm sad.*

*You laugh
at my jokes.*

*You call just to
see how I am.*

You compliment my new hairdo.

*You encourage me
to try new things.*

You don't send me stupid email jokes.

You tell me when you're worried about me.

You ask about my family, then listen to the response.

*You say no
to me at times.*

You know my favorite color.

You are concerned
about me when
I'm stressed or sick.

You tell me when you don't like an outfit I'm trying on in the store.

*You don't keep score
on which of us
did what when.*

You help me rearrange my heavy furniture.

*You rescue me when
my car breaks down.*

*You compliment
my cooking.*

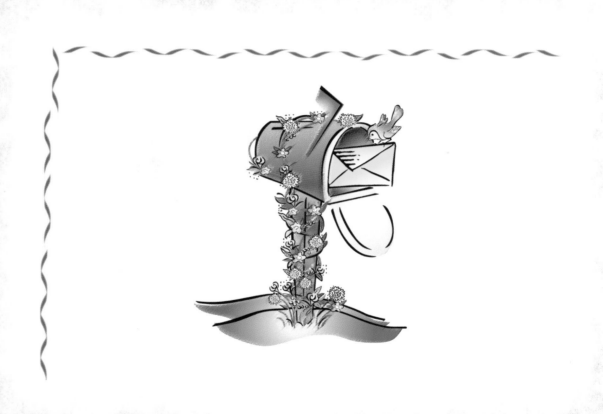

You send hand written thank you notes.

*You are
compassionate
to others.*

*You understand
why I gave
you this book.*

About the Author

Award winning author, columnist, speaker, and publisher, Sharron Stockhausen, MMA, CPCM, CAP, owns Stockhausen Ink, a speaking, training, and communication consulting business. She is also CEO of Expert Publishing, Inc. and one of the founders of the Expert Speakers Group. She holds a masters degree in management and administration, is a member of the National Speakers Association, National Speakers Association/Minnesota, the Midwest Independent Publishers Association, and the National Association of Women Business Owners. She teaches communication and management in the graduate and undergraduate programs at a university in Minnesota, and teaches business, speech, and writing at two other colleges. She lives with her husband in Minnesota.

About the Illustrator

Cindy Brueck, owner of The Sketch Pad in Burnsville, Minnesota, brings more than twenty years of experience as a graphic designer to this book. Her client list covers a variety of businesses, and her creativity has helped many companies build professional images, while helping authors offer visual impact to their words. She lives in rural Minnesota.